the Living Ocean

Spectacular Sharks

Bobbie Kalman & Molly Aloian
♣ Crabtree Publishing Company

www.crabtreebooks.com

the Living Ocean

Created by Bobbie Kalman

Dedicated by Molly Aloian
For my parents, Ken and Sharon. Your love means the world to me.

Editor-in-Chief
Bobbie Kalman

Writing team
Bobbie Kalman
Molly Aloian

Editorial director
Niki Walker

Editors
Amanda Bishop
Rebecca Sjonger
Kathryn Smithyman

Copy editor
Laura Hysert

Art director
Robert MacGregor

Design
Margaret Amy Reiach

Production coordinator
Heather Fitzpatrick

Photo research
Laura Hysert

Consultant
Patricia Loesche, Ph.D., Animal Behavior Program,
Department of Psychology, University of Washington

Photographs
Seapics.com: © Doug Perrine: pages 21, 31 (bottom);
© Doug Perrine/Jose Castro: page 11 (bottom right);
© James D. Watt: page 8; © Gary Bell: page 9 (top); © Mako Hirose: page 16 (top);
© Marty Snyderman: page 16 (bottom); © C & M Fallows: page 17 (top);
© Bob Cranston: page 19 (bottom); © Jim Robinson: page 26
Tom Stack & Associates: David B. Fleetham: pages 4, 11 (middle);
Brian Parker/Tom Stack: page 11 (bottom left)
Visuals Unlimited: Hal Beral: page 14 (top); James R. McCullagh: page 15 (bottom);
Marty Snyderman: pages 17 (bottom), 18 (bottom); Alex Kerstitch: pages 19 (top),
20 (top); Richard Herrmann: page 27 (top); David B. Fleetham: page 27 (bottom)
Jeffrey Rotman Photography: Jeff Rotman: pages 12 (top), 14 (bottom), 15 (top),
18 (top), 28, 29, 30 (top); Koji Nakamura: page 20 (bottom)
Other images by Digital Stock

Illustrations
Barbara Bedell: pages 5 (cladoselache, spiny dogfish, angel shark), 6, 7,
13 (lower top & bottom right), 15, 17, 19, 21, 24-25 (shimp, squid)
Margaret Amy Reiach: pages 13 (upper top and bottom left), 22, 23,
24-25 (background, ray, crab, barnacles, lobster, sea lion, octopus, clams, plankton)
Bonna Rouse: page 24-25 (sea turtle, shark, mackerel)
Katherine Kantor: page 5 (skate)
Cori Marvin: page 5 (stingray)

Crabtree Publishing Company

www.crabtreebooks.com   1-800-387-7650

PMB 16A
350 Fifth Avenue
Suite 3308
New York, NY
10118

612 Welland Avenue
St. Catharines
Ontario
Canada
L2M 5V6

73 Lime Walk
Headington
Oxford
OX3 7AD
United Kingdom

Cataloging-in-Publication Data
Kalman, Bobbie
   Spectacular sharks / Bobbie Kalman & Molly Aloian.
      p. cm. — (The Living ocean series)
This book examines the behavior, habitats, and bodies of these
prehistoric fish, dispels shark myths, and describes how they hunt,
why sharks are important to oceans, and why many are in danger.
   ISBN 0-7787-1298-2 (RLB) — ISBN 0-7787-1320-2 (pbk.)
   1. Sharks—Juvenile literature. [1. Sharks.] I. Aloian, Molly.
II. Title. III. Series.
   QL638.9.K36 2003
   597.3—dc21

2003004550
LC

JUL 0 7 2004

BW/

Contents

fascinating fish

Sharks are fish. They live underwater and take in oxygen through **gills**. Like most fish, sharks are **cold-blooded** animals. Their body temperatures change as the temperature of the water around them changes. When sharks swim in warm water, their body temperatures rise. In cool water, their body temperatures drop.

Fish are **vertebrates**, or animals with backbones. Most fish are **bony** fish. They have skeletons made up of hard bones. Sharks are **cartilaginous** fish. Their skeletons are made up of **cartilage**. Cartilage is a tough, flexible material that is lighter than bone. Lightweight cartilage makes it easy for sharks to move in water.

No reason to change

The first sharks lived on Earth more than 400 million years ago—before there were dinosaurs! Since that time, many types of animals have become **extinct**. When animals are extinct, they have disappeared from Earth forever. Ancient sharks survived because they became well **adapted**, or suited to, hunting and swimming in the oceans. Their bodies became so well adapted to ocean life that there was little reason for the bodies of later sharks to change much. Many of today's sharks have bodies that are similar to those of their **ancestors**.

cladoselache

spiny dogfish

The spiny dogfish is a modern shark. Its body is similar to that of its ancestor, cladoselache, which lived about 350 million years ago.

skate

stingray

angel shark

Shark relatives

Sharks are closely related to **skates** and **rays**. Together, these animals make up a group known as **elasmobranchs**. Like sharks, skates and rays are cartilaginous fish. They have wide, flat bodies and large, winglike fins. Their bodies resemble those of angel sharks.

Many different sharks

There are at least 375 **species**, or types, of sharks. Scientists organize them into eight major groups, called **orders**. Sharks in the same order may be different sizes or colors, but they are all alike in at least one way, such as having a similar body shape or the same number of fins. These pages show some members of each shark order.

Hexanchiformes

Frilled sharks and cow sharks make up this order. These sharks have more gills and fewer fins than other sharks do.

frilled shark

Squatiniformes

This order contains eighteen species of angel sharks, which have wide, flat bodies.

angel shark

Pristiophoriformes

This order is made up of five species of sawsharks. These sharks have flat snouts that resemble chainsaws.

sawshark

Squaliformes

The sharks in this order have slender bodies, narrow mouths, and powerful jaws.

Greenland sleeper shark

blackbelly lantern shark

Orectolobiformes

This order has the world's largest fish—the whale shark—as well as smaller sharks. Despite their differences in size, all of these sharks have one thing in common—their mouths are at the tip of their snouts.

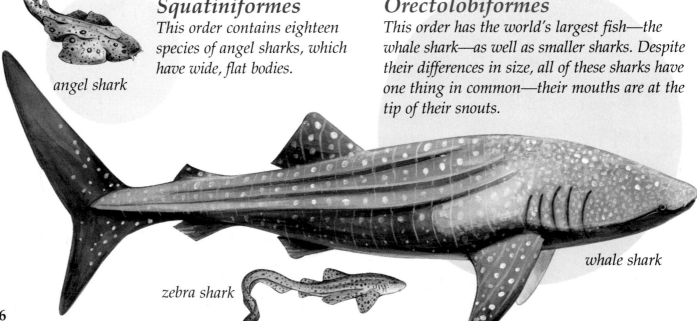

whale shark

zebra shark

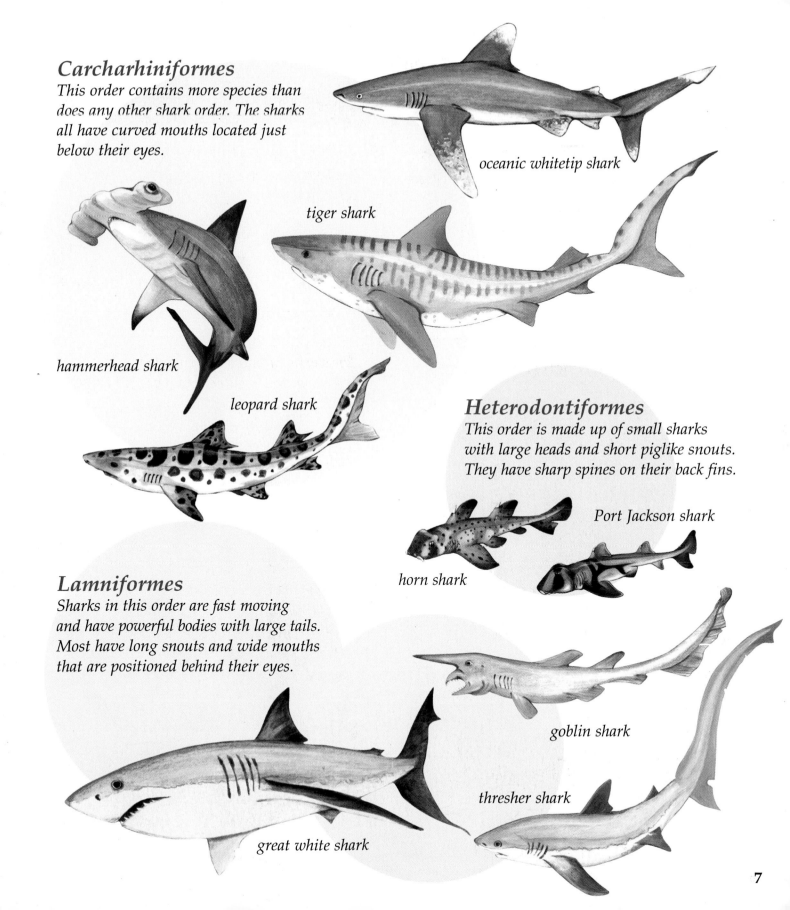

Carcharhiniformes

This order contains more species than does any other shark order. The sharks all have curved mouths located just below their eyes.

oceanic whitetip shark

tiger shark

hammerhead shark

leopard shark

Heterodontiformes

This order is made up of small sharks with large heads and short piglike snouts. They have sharp spines on their back fins.

Port Jackson shark

horn shark

Lamniformes

Sharks in this order are fast moving and have powerful bodies with large tails. Most have long snouts and wide mouths that are positioned behind their eyes.

goblin shark

thresher shark

great white shark

Where do sharks live?

Sharks live in all the world's oceans, except in the freezing waters around Antarctica. Some species live in warm waters, and others live in cold waters. They are found at various depths of the ocean.

Some sharks stay in either deep or shallow water, whereas others move from one depth to another. All sharks need salt water to survive, but a few species can swim into freshwater rivers and lakes.

Different habitats

Sharks live in a variety of ocean **habitats**, or natural environments. Some, such as whale sharks, spend most of their time far from shore, swimming in sunlit waters near the ocean's surface. Others, such as frilled sharks, live in the dark, cold depths. Many sharks, including the gray reef sharks shown left, cruise in warm, coastal waters near coral reefs. In these warm areas, sharks are sometimes found in lagoons and **estuaries** as well. Some sharks, such as horn sharks and angel sharks, live mainly on rocky or sandy ocean floors.

Ornate wobbegongs rest on the ocean's rocky bottom during the day.

On the move

Many sharks **migrate**, or travel long distances, at certain times of the year. Sharks migrate for a variety of reasons: to follow **prey**, to find warmer or cooler waters, and to seek safe spots where they can **reproduce**, or make babies. Blue sharks make the longest known journey of any shark. They travel in the Atlantic Ocean between the northeastern United States and Brazil—a trip of up to 1,700 miles (2735 km)!

Many sharks live solitary lives, but some, such as these hammerheads, swim in schools, or groups.

Water bodies

All shark bodies are made up of the same basic parts, but sharks do not all look the same. They come in different sizes, shapes, and colors depending on their species, where they live, and how they hunt (see pages 16-17). There are two main types of shark bodies, however. Sharks that are **active swimmers** have **streamlined**, or sleekly shaped, bodies and powerful fins that allow them to move easily through water. Sharks that are **bottom dwellers** have wide, flat bodies that are suited to lying on the ocean floor.

A shark's body

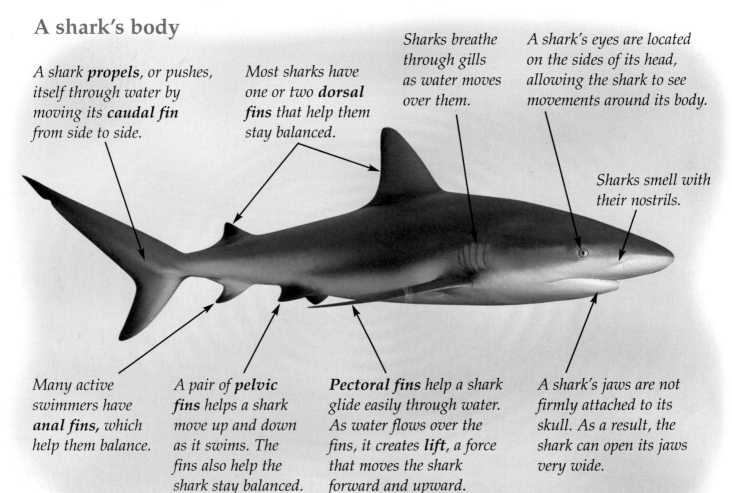

*A shark **propels**, or pushes, itself through water by moving its **caudal fin** from side to side.*

*Most sharks have one or two **dorsal fins** that help them stay balanced.*

Sharks breathe through gills as water moves over them.

A shark's eyes are located on the sides of its head, allowing the shark to see movements around its body.

Sharks smell with their nostrils.

*Many active swimmers have **anal fins,** which help them balance.*

*A pair of **pelvic fins** helps a shark move up and down as it swims. The fins also help the shark stay balanced.*

***Pectoral fins** help a shark glide easily through water. As water flows over the fins, it creates **lift**, a force that moves the shark forward and upward.*

A shark's jaws are not firmly attached to its skull. As a result, the shark can open its jaws very wide.

Lighter than water

Sharks have huge livers filled with oil, which is lighter than water. The oil in their livers makes the sharks lighter in the water, allowing them to swim more easily. A few species, such as sand tiger sharks, also gulp air to make themselves lighter.

As the blue shark swims fast, a lot of water passes over its gills, providing the shark with plenty of oxygen.

Sink or swim

Active swimmers rarely stop moving. If they did, they would slowly sink because their bodies are too heavy to float. They also have to swim to breathe. As these sharks move, water flows over their gills and they **absorb**, or take in, oxygen from it.

spiracle

Water pumpers

Bottom-dwelling sharks do not have to move constantly in order to breathe. They can pump water over their gills by opening and closing their mouths. These sharks also have holes, called **spiracles**, behind their eyes that draw oxygen from the water and carry it to their gills.

Tough stuff

Sharks may appear to have smooth skin, but their skin is actually rough like sandpaper. It is covered with toothlike scales called **denticles**. Denticles help protect sharks. They are sharp enough to injure animals that rub against them! Denticles also help sharks move through the water by **channeling**, or moving, water over their bodies.

nurse shark denticles

Greenland sleeper shark denticles

Sensational senses

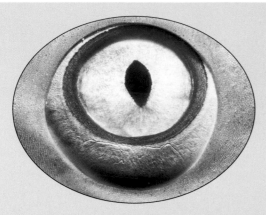

*A shark has a special layer, called a **tapetum lucidum**, at the back of each eye. This layer reflects light to the shark's eyes, which helps the shark see at night or in deep, dark water.*

Many sharks, including the blue shark above, can smell a single drop of blood in a million drops of water.

Sharks are excellent **predators**, or hunters, because of their sharp senses. Most sharks not only have keen senses of smell, sight, hearing, and taste, but they also have special senses that they use just for finding food. Prey does not often escape the attention of a hungry shark!

Smelling the ocean

Sharks have such an excellent sense of smell that they are often called "swimming noses." Many sharks can smell animals or blood—a sign of easy-to-catch, injured prey—from miles away! A shark smells with its nostrils, which are on either side of its snout. The position of its nostrils helps the shark locate the scent. If a smell hits its left nostril first, the shark knows to head left in search of prey. Hungry sharks often swim in zig-zag patterns, moving their heads from side to side in search of a scent to follow. This way of swimming helps sharks find prey quickly.

Getting the vibe

A shark has a **lateral line**, which is a row of fluid-filled tubes that runs along both sides of its head and body. The lateral line helps the shark sense the movements of nearby animals. The movements create **vibrations**, or tiny ripples of water, which are felt by the lateral line. The lateral line can help a shark locate prey that is as far away as 100 yards (91 m). A shark can also feel ocean currents with its lateral line, helping it sense the direction in which it is headed.

A shark uses its lateral line to track the sound of an injured animal struggling in the water. Sound travels through water as ripples that the shark can feel.

Sensing electricity

All living creatures give off small electrical charges. A shark has an area in its head, known as the **ampullae of Lorenzini**, that senses these charges. Charges are picked up by tiny pits in the skin of a shark's snout. Sharks can feel charges from up to three feet (0.9 m) away. They follow a prey's electricity when they move in to bite.

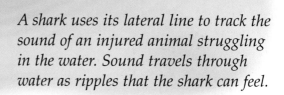

13

feeding habits

Sharks feed on a wide variety of prey, including all kinds of fish, lobsters, crabs, shrimps, squids, octopuses, sea birds, seals, and sea lions. Large sharks often hunt and eat smaller sharks. Some sharks also feed on **carrion**, or dead animals. They may even eat sea plants and trash that has been dumped in the ocean.

Sharks that feed on small fish may need to eat twice a day to get enough food. Sharks that eat larger prey, such as seals or sea turtles, may need to feed only once or twice a week.

Not over-eaters

Although sharks have reputations for eating nonstop, they eat only enough food to survive. Most sharks eat one large meal every two or three days. Some sharks can survive without eating for weeks or even months by living off the oil stored in their large livers. The amount of food a shark eats depends on how much it moves. Active swimmers such as blue sharks eat more food than do bottom dwellers such as nurse sharks. Active swimmers are also able to digest their food more quickly than bottom dwellers can.

Some sharks, including the whitetip reef sharks above, hunt in large groups at night. Others feed alone during the day.

Gulp!

Sharks do not chew their food the way people do. When feeding on large prey, sharks tear off chunks of flesh and swallow them in big gulps.

Sharks swallow small prey whole, as the whitetip reef shark above is about to do. Large sharks can also swallow big prey whole. Tiger sharks have been known to swallow squids in one gulp!

Filtering food

Basking sharks, whale sharks, and megamouth sharks are some of the largest sharks, but they feed on the smallest prey! These sharks eat tiny fish, shrimp, and microscopic plants and animals called **plankton**. The sharks are **filter feeders**, which means they eat by swimming with their mouths open and **filtering**, or straining, their prey from the water.

*This basking shark is filtering its meal from the water with special mouth parts called **gill rakers**.*

On the hunt

Every type of shark uses a specific hunting method to catch prey. For instance, fast-swimming sharks chase their prey, whereas slow-moving sharks wait for prey to swim nearby before they strike.

Bottom-dwelling sharks, including wobbegongs and angel sharks, are known as "ambush predators" because they hide and catch their prey by surprise. These sharks have **camouflage**, or colors and markings that help them blend in with their surroundings. Camouflage allows them to lie hidden on the ocean floor to wait for prey, which often swims right up to them. When prey gets close, the sharks pop up and snatch it with their teeth.

When a fish, octopus, or snail swims close, this angel shark bursts from the sand and bites the prey with its needle-like teeth.

Finding buried treasure

Some bottom-dwelling sharks, such as the sawshark shown right, have sensitive **barbels** that hang down on both sides of their long snouts. These sharks use their barbels to scan the sand for buried prey. When they find prey, the sharks use their snouts to disturb it and then snatch it.

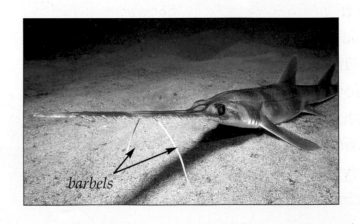

barbels

Chasing down prey

Great whites and blue sharks are active swimmers that rely on their speed while hunting. These sharks are so quick that they often overtake fast-moving prey such as seals and tuna. The sharks are capable of great bursts of speed because they can raise their temperatures slightly. A warmer body temperature can make these sharks stronger and faster than they normally would be. A great white shark can gain so much speed that it can even **breach**, or jump out of the water, to grab a seabird or seal from the surface, as shown right.

*Many sharks have **countershading**, or dark backs and light bellies. Countershading helps them sneak up on prey. Animals above them may not see the sharks' black or gray backs against the dark water below. From below, prey may not see the sharks' white or pale gray bellies against the ocean's sunlit surface.*

thresher shark

Bump and slash

Many large sharks, including great whites and tiger sharks, often use sneak attacks to capture their prey so that they do not have to chase it. They strike their prey from behind and below. Some sharks bump prey with their snouts. This action stuns the prey long enough for the sharks to take a bite. The thresher shark, shown above, has a unique hunting method. It herds fish into a tight group by swimming in smaller and smaller circles around them. It then lashes them with its tail to stun or kill them.

*Some sharks, including the blue shark above, have **nictitating membranes** to cover their eyes. When the sharks attack, the membranes slide up to protect their eyes from slashing or biting prey.*

The size and shape of a shark's teeth are suited to what it eats and how it eats. Depending on its species, a shark's teeth can be large or small, pointy or blunt, and jagged like a saw or smooth like a razor blade.

Custom-made teeth

Many bottom-dwelling sharks feed on crabs, lobsters, and other shelled animals. They have small peglike teeth for cracking and grinding the shells of their prey. Active sharks often feed on large prey such as whales, seals, and sea lions. They have triangular teeth with sawlike edges for slashing and biting chunks out of their prey. Sharks that feed on slippery prey, such as squids, often have needle-like teeth to puncture and hold their prey.

Upper and lower

Some sharks have totally different types of teeth on their upper and lower jaws. These sharks usually feed on slippery prey. For instance, dusky sharks have long, thin teeth on their upper jaws and wide, sharp teeth on their lower jaws. When a dusky shark catches a slippery ray, the lower teeth hold the prey while the upper teeth cut it.

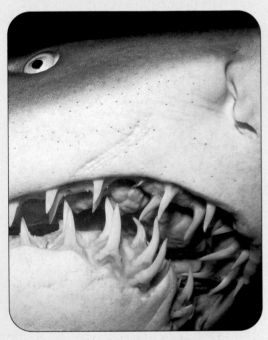

The sand tiger shark has long, narrow teeth that curve toward its throat to grab and hold slippery prey such as octopus or squid.

The leopard shark's teeth have sharp, narrow tips for biting fish, crabs, and clams.

Unlimited teeth

Unlike most animals, sharks have more than one row of teeth. They have up to seven rows! When a tooth falls out, the one behind it moves forward to replace it. Some types of sharks can lose a whole row of teeth in ten days. Others keep their teeth for up to a year. A shark may lose more than 30,000 teeth in its lifetime!

Sharp and ready

Sharks lose their teeth easily because the teeth are not attached to the jaws with roots. Sharks often lose teeth while grabbing prey, but teeth also fall out when they are old and worn out. Since sharks replace their teeth constantly, they always have a sharp new set ready to grab and cut prey.

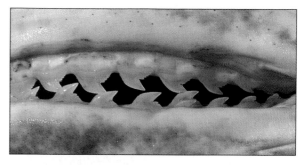

The L-shaped teeth of tiger sharks easily slice through prey. They are even sharp enough to pry open the shells of sea turtles.

Nurse sharks lose their teeth often, but they have thousands of replacement teeth lined up.

Jaw power

Some shark species, including great whites, have jaws that are attached to their skulls by strong, stretchy muscles. When the sharks open their mouths to bite prey, the jaws move forward. The sharks can then bite the prey without their snouts getting in the way.

As the shark approaches its prey, it raises its head and drops its lower jaw.

The upper jaw is pushed out of the mouth while the lower jaw moves forward and up.

The upper jaw comes down and finishes the bite, slicing a chunk from the prey.

Baby sharks

Male and female sharks of the same species **mate** in order to reproduce. All baby sharks, or **pups**, grow inside eggs and feed off **yolk sacs**. Some sharks lay their eggs, and others carry them inside their bodies. Compared to other fish, sharks have very few babies Some have only two babies in a **litter**.

This swell shark embryo is attached to a yolk sac, which provides the embryo with the nutrients it needs to grow.

This baby shark is almost out of its case. It used its denticles, fins, and tail to hatch.

Safe on the outside

Some female sharks lay their eggs in tough protective cases. They search for hidden spots on the ocean floor on which to leave these cases. For instance, zebra sharks attach their egg cases to corals or rocks. An **embryo**, or developing shark, stays inside its egg case until it is fully formed.

Safe on the inside

Most female sharks, including whale sharks, tiger sharks, and great whites, do not lay eggs. Instead, the females carry their eggs inside their bodies until the pups are ready to hatch. The pups tear out of their eggs and then leave their mothers' bodies and swim away.

Connected to mom

Some embryos, including those of lemon and hammerhead sharks, are fed by both yolk sacs and their mothers' bodies. As a pup grows inside its mother's body, its yolk sac slowly runs out of food and turns into a **placenta**. The placenta connects the pup to its mother's body and allows extra nutrients and oxygen to pass from her body to the growing pup.

Only the strongest hatch

The pups of a few species, including sand tiger sharks and thresher sharks, begin their fight to survive while they are still inside their mothers! One or two eggs develop faster and hatch sooner than the others do. The newly hatched young then feed on the eggs around them and grow even stronger before they leave their mothers' bodies.

Most baby sharks grow for seven to ten months before they are ready to hatch or leave their mothers' bodies. A few take almost a year to develop. All pups are able to swim and hunt for themselves immediately.

When sharks attack

Many people dislike sharks because they fear being attacked. The truth is that sharks are more likely to avoid than to attack people. Of the hundreds of species of sharks, only about ten have been known to bite humans. People also fear sharks because they do not know why sharks attack. Although some attacks do seem to happen for no reason, many happen for reasons that are clear once people understand how sharks behave.

Scientists often wear metal mesh suits when approaching sharks to study why they bite.

Most types of sharks do not bother divers as long as the people respect the animals' space.

Mistaken identity

Some attacks seem to occur because sharks mistake people for prey. Many of these attacks happen in shallow, murky water, where sharks may confuse splashing swimmers for injured prey. In these attacks, sharks usually bite once and then swim away. Some scientists believe that great whites attack surfers because, from below, surfers paddling on their boards resemble seals or sea lions.

seal

surfer

Feeling threatened

It may seem hard to believe that a person could frighten a shark, but some attacks happen for that reason. When divers or swimmers accidentally step on sleeping nurse sharks or other bottom-dwelling sharks, the animals may bite in self-defense. Without even realizing it, people can threaten sharks by getting too close to the animals. Cornered sharks may attack out of fear. Sometimes people deliberately provoke attacks by trying to touch or grab sharks!

Back off!

Gray reef sharks are known to warn divers and swimmers with displays before they attack. A gray reef shark that feels threatened swims slowly and stiffly in a figure-eight pattern. It arches its back and points its pectoral fins down. It also raises its snout and opens its jaws a little. When divers or swimmers see a gray reef shark behaving this way, they should swim away slowly and steadily.

23

Part of the web

All living things need food energy to survive. Plants can make their own food, but animals cannot. They must eat plants or other animals to get energy. The pattern of eating and being eaten is called a **food chain**. The arrows below show where energy moves along food chains. When an animal feeds on a variety of other animals, it links several food chains and forms a **food web**.

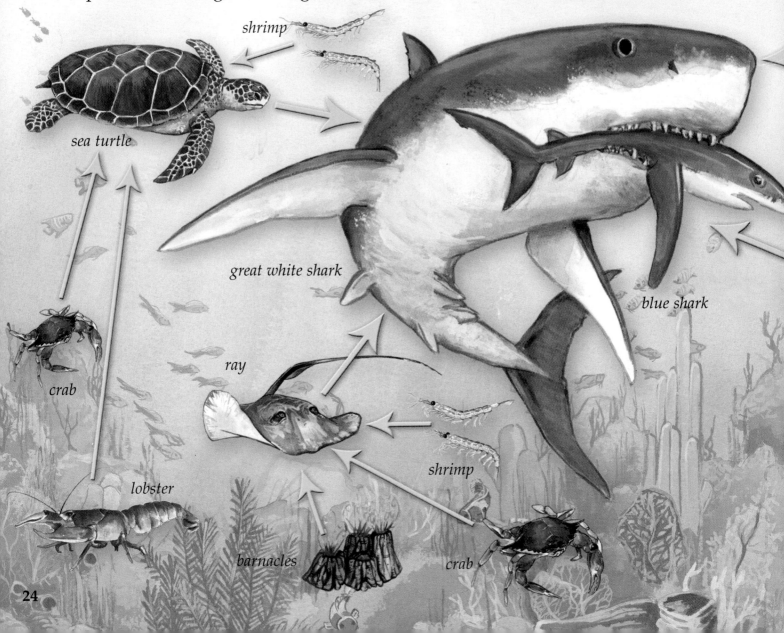

shrimp

sea turtle

great white shark

blue shark

crab

ray

lobster

shrimp

barnacles

crab

Top of the chain

Large sharks are **apex predators**. They are at the **apex**, or top, of many ocean food chains. They are important because they help keep food webs balanced. If the population of a species grows, apex predators hunt more of those animals and bring their numbers back to normal.

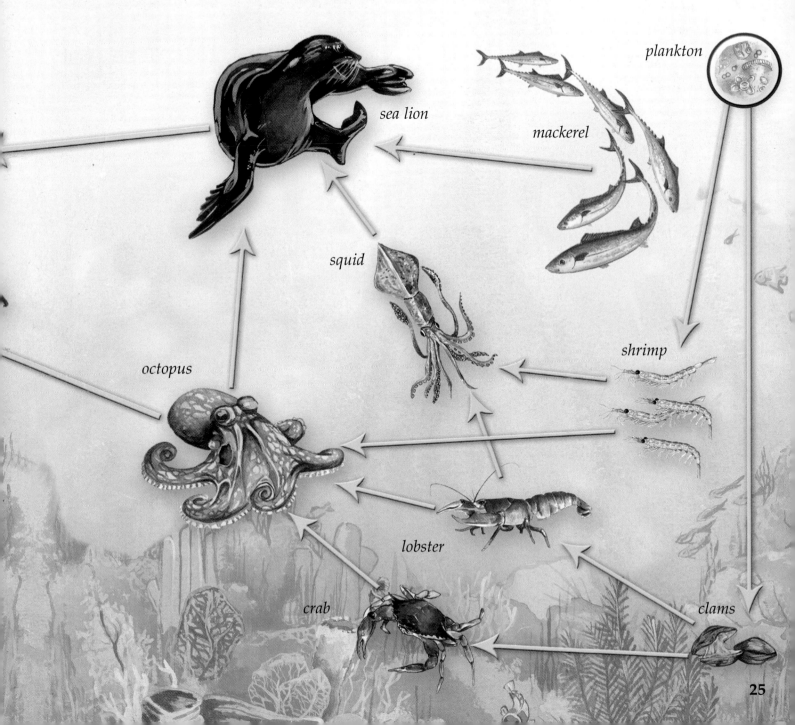

plankton

sea lion

mackerel

squid

octopus

shrimp

lobster

crab

clams

Keeping the balance

Sharks are an important part of ocean **ecosystems** such as the coral reef above. An ecosystem is made up of plants, animals, and nonliving natural things such as sand and rocks. Sharks help keep ocean ecosystems healthy by eating animals that are weak, sick, or injured. Hunting these animals keeps populations strong and healthy because the weakest animals are removed. Sharks also feed on carrion, which helps keep oceans clean. If too many dead animals were left in the ocean, the environment would become **septic**, or rotten. In a septic ocean, many animals would become sick and die.

Balanced numbers

Sharks help maintain the balance of prey and predator populations in ocean food chains and webs. Apex predators are especially important, since they affect everything below them in the food chains. They keep populations of other predators, such as large fish, octopuses, seals, and whales, from growing too large. If sharks disappeared from food webs, these populations would grow. Their food supply would remain the same, however, and there would be an imbalance in the food web. The predators would quickly wipe out their food sources, and some of them would starve. Other animals that relied on the same food sources would also starve. The effects of this imbalance would move throughout the food web.

Attached to sharks

Some sharks are especially helpful to small fish called remoras, which attach themselves to sharks with special suckers. The two small fish swimming with this reef shark are remoras. These fish not only get a free ride and protection from predators, but they also get leftover bits of the shark's food. Scientists are not sure whether sharks benefit from remoras.

Threats to sharks

People are the biggest threat to sharks. Humans kill more than 100 million sharks a year. Many are caught for their meat by commercial fisheries. Some people kill sharks just for their dorsal fins, which are considered a gourmet food in some parts of the world. They cut off the fins and toss the animals back into the ocean, where they are unable to move. The sharks eventually bleed to death. A lot of shark populations are now **endangered**, or in danger of dying out, due to overfishing. Every year, thousands of sharks are also caught by accident as **bycatch**. They get tangled in large fishing nets that are meant to trap other species of fish such as tuna or anchovies. The trapped sharks are not able to swim or hunt, and they eventually die. Blue sharks, oceanic whitetip sharks, and thresher sharks are just a few of the species that get killed as bycatch.

Shark fins are dried and sold for a lot of money. They are used to make shark-fin soup, which is an expensive food in some countries.

Cartilage and liver

Some sharks are killed for their livers and cartilage. Shark-liver oil is used in some brands of vitamins as a source of vitamin A. **Squalene,** which is found in the livers of deep-water sharks, is an ingredient used in some cosmetics. Doctors sometimes use shark cartilage to help their patients heal after surgery. Many people take pills made of shark cartilage, believing that it helps cure infections or diseases such as arthritis and cancer. There is no scientific proof that these pills work.

Slow to grow

Sharks grow slowly and take many years to become **mature**, or ready to reproduce. Some are not mature until they are ten or fifteen years old. When they do reproduce, sharks do not have as many babies as other fish do. Due to overfishing, sharks are being killed faster than they reproduce. As a result, their populations are shrinking fast. Today many species of sharks, including great whites, dusky sharks, sand tiger sharks, and basking sharks, are in danger of being wiped out.

Learning about sharks

In recent years, scientsists have learned a lot about sharks and their behavior. They have even discovered new species of sharks! The more people learn about sharks, the more they realize how amazing these animals are and how important they are to the health of oceans.

Long, healthy lives

Many scientists believe that sharks are the hardiest ocean animals. Sharks rarely develop infections or diseases such as cancer. They also heal quickly when they are injured by other animals. Some scientists want to learn how shark **immune systems** work. With this knowledge, they hope to find ways of improving the immune systems of people.

Much to learn

Sharks are difficult to study, but scientists are always trying to learn more about them. They want to know how sharks behave, how fast they grow, how they interact with one another, and how many sharks live in various areas. You can help sharks by learning as much as you can about them. Start with these websites:

- www.sharks.org
- www.elasmo-research.org
- www.oceanofk.org/sharks/sharks

Sharks live much longer than most fish do. This whitetip reef shark may live up to 25 years.

Sharks in captivity

It is difficult to study sharks in the wild, so some sharks are captured to be studied in aquariums. Aquariums are not ideal places for sharks or the people studying them, however. The sharks do not behave as they would in the wild—they cannot swim long distances, hunt, or reproduce.

Most great white sharks do not survive very long in aquariums.

Sharks up close

Cage diving is one way that scientists and photographers can observe sharks in the wild. This method is especially useful for studying large sharks and sharks that are feeding. Divers are lowered in cages made of steel bars, which protect them from shark bites. They can then safely add blood or meat to the water to watch how sharks react. They can also study how sharks move and how they react to other sharks.

Playing tag

Tagging sharks allows scientists to track the animals from place to place and from year to year. A tag is a small plug with a radio **transmitter**, which a diver attaches under a shark's dorsal fin. It sends signals that scientists can interpret to learn the depth and temperature of the water in which the shark swims, how much the shark grows, and when and how far it migrates.

This scientist is tagging a tiger shark. Sharks are usually restrained with nets or ropes before scientists try to tag them.

Glossary

Note: Boldfaced words that are defined in the book may not appear in the glossary.

active swimmer A shark with a streamlined body that moves nonstop

ancestor An ancient relative

bottom dweller A shark with a wide, flat body that lives near or on the ocean floor

estuary A body of water that is a mix of salt water and fresh water, formed where a river meets an ocean

gill An organ with which sharks remove oxygen from the water

immune system Organs, tissues, and cells that work together to keep the body healthy

litter A group of shark pups that are born at the same time

mate To come together to make babies

mature Describing an adult animal that is able to make babies

predator An animal that hunts and eats other animals for food

prey An animal that is hunted and eaten by another animal

streamlined Describing a sleekly shaped body that slips easily through water

transmitter A piece of electronic equipment that sends signals to satellites and allows scientists to track the location of animals

yolk sac A small bag inside an egg that contains the yolk on which an embryo feeds

Index

1 2 3 4 5 6 7 8 9 0   Printed in the U.S.A.   2 1 0 9 8 7 6 5 4 3